HEINEMANN FRONTLINE SERIES
Midlife
Niyi Osundare

Niyi Osundare was born in Ikere-Ekiti, Ondo State of Nigeria in 1947; had his secondary education at Amoye Grammar School, Ikere, and Christ's School, Ado-Ekiti. He later graduated with a B.A. (Honours) in English from the University of Ibadan in 1972; M.A. from the University of Leeds in 1974; and Ph. D. from York University, Toronto.
Currently Senior Lecturer in English at the University of Ibadan, Osundare who teaches Creative Writing, Stylistics, Sociology of Language and Literature, is also a literary critic and well-known social commentator in Nigeria. He is a columnist for *Newswatch* magazine. He has been Fulbright Scholar at the University of Wisconsin-Madison, and Associate Professor of African and Caribbean Literature at the University of New Orleans.

Undoubtedly one of Africa's leading poets, Niyi Osundare is widely published in local and international magazines and journals. He has performed his poetry in several parts of the world, and his poems have been translated into Dutch, German, French, and Korean. Since 1985, he has run a weekly poetry column in the *Sunday Tribune*. His published volumes of poetry include *Songs of the Marketplace* (1983); *Village Voices* (1984); *The Eye of the Earth* (1986); *Moonsongs* (1988); *Waiting Laughters*, (1990); *Selected Poems* (1992). He had also written two unpublished plays one of which was performed in 1979 as one of the major events marking 20 Years of Television in Africa.

Among Osundare's numerous awards and prizes are: Association of Nigerian Authors Poetry Prize; Commonwealth Poetry Prize: the Cadbury Poetry Prize; and the Noma Award, Africa's most prestigious book award.

OTHER HEINEMANN FRONTLINERS

Upper Level

Cyprian Ekwensi: *For A Roll of Parchment*
Patrick Fagbola: *Kaduna Mafia*
Niyi Osundare: *The Eye of the Earth* (Joint-Winner of the 1986 Commonwealth Poetry Prize)
Rose Njoku: *Withstand the Storm*
Jeremiah Essien: *In the Shadow of Death*
Okinba Launko: *Minted Coins* (Winner of the Africa Zone of 1988 Dillions Commonwealth Poetry Prize)
Chinua Achebe: *Anthills of the Savannah*
Tess Onwueme: *The Reign of Wazobia and Other Plays*
Atabo Oko: *The Secret of the Sheik*
Tess Onwueme: *Legacies* (a play)
Niyi Osundare: *Songs of the Season* (poems)
Afolabi A Adio-Moses: *Flashes of Ideas and Reflections* (poems)
Telu Ajayi: *The Ghost of a Millionaire*
Oladele Akadiri: *A Sin in the Convent*
Bridget Nwankwo: *Drums of Destiny*
Iyorwuese H. Hagher: *Mulkin Mata* (a play)
Sola Osofisan: *Darksongs* (Winner 1990 ANA Poetry Prize)
Sola Osofisan: *The Living and The Dead* (Winner 1990 ANA Prose Prize)
Femi Osofisan: *Once Upon Four Robbers* (a play)
Stella Oyedepo: *Beyond the Dark Tunnel* (a play)
Chukwuemeka Ike: *The Search*
Chukwuemeka Ike: *The Naked Gods*
Chukwuemeka Ike: *The Chicken Chasers*
Stella Oyedepo: *The Greatest Gift*
ANA/ British Council: *Five Plays* (Winner 1989 ANA Drama Prize)
Patrick Idahosa: *Truth and Tragedy*
Chidi Ikonne: *Our Land*
Rasheed Gbadamosi: *Sunset Over Nairobi*
Femi Osofisan: *Aringindin and the Nightwatchmen*
Omowunmi Segun: *The Third Dimple* (Winner 1991 ANA Prose Prize)

Intermediate Level
 Chinelo Achebe: *The Last Laugh & Other Stories*
 Tess Onwueme: *Ban Empty Barn and Other Plays*
 Catherine Acholonu: *The Trial of the Beautiful Ones*
 S. Arogbofa: *Agidi Sours* (a play)
 Ola Rotimi: *If: A Tragedy of the Ruled* (a play)
 F. Aig-Imoukhuede: *Pidgin Stew and Sufferhead*
 Kathleen Egbuna: *That Wartime*
 Tony Marinho: *The Epidemic*

Junior Level
 A.O. Oyekanmi: *The Lion and the Hare*
 Augustus Adebayo: *Once Upon a Village*
 Chinua Achebe: *Chike and the River*
 Cyprian Ekwensi: *Gone to Mecca*
 Chinwe M Agbakoba: *Mma and Nkita*
 Chinwe M Agbakoba: *Ejiofor and His Mother*
 Margaret Brook: *The Play for Yejide*
 Cyprian Ekwensi: *Passport of Mallam Ilia*
 Cyprian Ekwensi: *Trouble in Form Six*
 Chio Enwonwu: *Tortoise in Exile*
 Chio Enwonwu: *Tortoise Goes to Town*
 Chio Enwonwu: *Tortoise Returns to the Woods*
 Ernest Emenyonu: *Uzo Remembers His Father*
 Chinua Achebe & John Iroaganachi: *How the Leopard Got Its Claws*
 Olufunmilayo Oyelese: *Where is the Princess?*
 Gabriel Okara: *An Adventure to Juju Island*
 Gabriel Okara: *Little Snake and Little Frog*

Midlife

Niyi Osundare

Heinemann Educational Books (Nigeria) PLC

HEINEMANN EDUCATIONAL BOOKS (NIGERIA) PLC
Head Office: 1 Ighodaro Road, Jericho, P.M.B. 5205, Ibadan
Phone: 417060 & 417061; *Telex:* 31113 HEBOOKS NG
Cable: HEBOOK Ibadan

Area Offices and Branches
Abeokuta . Akure . Bauchi . Benin City . Calabar . Enugu . Ibadan
Ikeja . Ilorin . Jos . Kano . Katsina . Maiduguri . Makurdi . Minna
Owerri . Port Harcourt . Sokoto . Uyo . Yola . Zaria

© Niyi Osundare 1993
First published 1993

ISBN 978 129 198 2

All Rights Reserved

No part of this publication may be reproduced, stored in a retrieval system or transmitted in any form or by any means, electronic, mechanical, photocopying, recording, or otherwise, without the prior permission of Heinemann Educational Books (Nigeria) PLC.
 This book is sold subject to the condition that it should not by way of trade or otherwise be lent, re-sold, hired out or otherwise circulated without the publisher's prior consent in any form of binding or cover other than that in which it is published and without a similar condition including this condition being imposed on the subsequent purchaser.

Printed by W. Girardet Press (W.A.) Co., Yemetu, Ibadan

Dedication

To   The wonderful staff of the International Writing Program,
University of Iowa, Iowa City, U.S.A.

To   Syl, Tong-Choon, Celso, Angelica, Zsuzsa, Sasha, Birgir,
Elsa, Filipe, Nonilon and other members of the 1988 I.W.P.

And, most gratefully,
to Kemi my wife,
and Moyo, Tola,
and Bayonle, our little ones,
who held the home front while this battle of songs
raged on the busy banks of the Iowa River.

...... the verse that kneads
Abandoned clay, and brings to pulse
The dreamt feast of all humanity.

                              Wole Soyinka

Every language I love, of all peoples and lands,
All that is honest in them and humane.

                              Gervog Emin

I shall bring the light for the world
I shall bring warmth for mankind.

                              Ai Qing

I am large, I contain multitudes

                              Walt Whitman

Foreline

Midlife. Noontide in the diary of the sun. Dawn has raced quietly by, twilight peeps in from a compass of looming shadows. Past forty now, the riddling kola of life ripening, ripening in my mouth, a few grey strands keep on surprising the thicket of the head. Taller too, able to look the giant in the face, able to ask Africa a few sunny questions about her dormant dawn. Able to ask the world how many wasted nights really make up a single day.

Midlife. Noontide. The sun rules the universe of these songs. The sun, from the fertile rocks of my ancient origins whose noonlit river thrives with dappled shoals. The rocks are my bones, the river my fluent veins. And the valley where both meet in clod and clay, that valley moulds the legend of my flesh.

Midcourse now, equidistant between heady mountains and the waiting sea ...

And questions tumble down like cataracts of upland banters: how old has the world grown in my span of being, how young; how many creases on the brow of the rock; how much deeper the navel of the road; how has the sea counted its drops of water; how many bridges have creaked under my wondering feet; how many fruits have I plucked from the tree of laughter; how many mares of sorrow have galloped down my tearful face; how large the conquistador's sword, how crimson the plunder of the atom?

Midlife, I ask the mountain, I ask the valley, I ask the earthworm which softens the soil for the blossom of tall harvests: the dream so fervently pledged in the garden of our dawn, when will it bloom?

This volume, therefore, is informed by an inescapably panoramic vision where voices are many, protean, even kaleidoscopic. In keeping with the oral poetic tradition whose inexhaustible lifespring I am forever indebted to, poetry here is confession, declaration, reflection, play, struggle, vision ... It is exchange, an unwavering engagement with the world, a dynamic treasury of noetic probings and rooted voyagings mediated through epic syntax and experimentation in the choric blend of rhetoric and song.

Midlife. The boulder plucked off its upland base has suffered life's long river till midcourse. The world I see is bent.

I am mode and medium for its straightening.

Iowa City, Ibadan   Niyi Osundare
1988   1989

Contents

Page

Foreline.. ix

I
Rocksong.. 1

II
What the River said... 16

III
Human in every sense....................................... 33

IV
Breaking walls.. 63

V
Diary of the sun.. 71

VI
Midlife... 87

VII
Thread in the loom.. 101

1
Rocksong

I
am a caller at noon
restless sphere of the universe of the sun,
of galloping oceans and rocks
which bathe their feet in misty waters,
of the sky's blue, blue teeth
and clouds which gather the promise of rain

I am light
I am shadow
I am the luminous covenant
Of short and tall spaces

I am the eye's mid-wink
in an orchard of visions,
depths which find their name
in the register of brightening dials

I am the green rhumba of the forest,
of tapping roots, and twigs
swaying, swaying to the promptings
of the wind,
an echo passed tree to tree
like a legend of whispering idioms;
I am the amber sheen of coconut leaves
rasping, rapping in the theatre
of the breeze,
the long hard journey from crust to core

I am the lustre of the river
in the swollen plenitude of August;

banks which count their coins
in shadows of rapid showers

I am a caller at noon;
I have cut my teeth
at the elbow of the moon;
ripening cornfields drive no fear
into the mouth of my sun

I am a caller at noon.

ii

First,
Noon spoke
in visions of measured torrent:

>turkeys' wattle, larynx of the wind
>ant's intestine, echoes of silence
>
>clumsy pincers of the crab
>oracle of seven-lobed kola
>
>tattooed biceps of open books
>archives of crunchy proverbs
>
>the forest's inky depth
>footfalls of galloping mountains
>
>the millipede's many-legged race
>patience of noonward hoofs
>
>the parrot's rear plumage
>the sunflower's dial-petalled bunch
>
>the equator's dark accent
>stitch of broken suns
>
>purple sperm of the flame
>blue stanza in the song of the star
>
>fragments of fancy
>map of journeying skies

the stone's murmur
eloquence of blunt sickles

the tyrant's testicle
labia of pouting guns

monodies of cleansing iron
cleansing iron, cleansing iron

monodies of cleansing iron

I am a caller at noon

iii

Through burning waters
Through ashes of accumulated patience
Through earth which chews the showers
of tardy rains
Through lakes pregnant with storms
Through seasons which bloom every seed
For twilights of contending baskets
Through earth's gable
Through the window of the sky

    The sun reaches out for its ram horn*

Waiting noons are auricles of radiant blarings;
my memory now is a tale of a thousand masks
I am a caller at noon.
I look the sun, my sun
in the face
and I harvest colours of unnameable depths
where sowing, once dew, now sweat,
is shade for a million temples.
Light is my promise
my shadow hemless ripple
of the ocean's abiding loom.

The seed, once dew, now sweat,
the dripping clay of the first light
has hardened into a polished porcelain
of thickening shadows

---

*   Ram-horn: the visionary's medium, used for calling tunes and for rallying good will.

I am light
I am shadow
I am the luminous covenant
Of short and tall spaces

I am a caller at noon

iv

Child of the river, child of the rock
child of the delicate boulder
of the beginning,
of burning quarries and flames
of eloquent clay

Cinders of the first fire
cinders, of the first scarlet sprinkle
and murmurs of parting mists,
of the telling legacy of the blaze
which swallowed the night,
spitting flint and flair
in paths of hardening lores

> The boulder is father of the rock
> The boulder is father of the rock
> Swift-footed courier of the craggy acre
> The egg which crows the tale
> In cradles of ashen dawns ...

And, sizzling from the sun,
from the first blue touch of the waiting sea
the boulder cools its fine-grained heels
in the liquid mercy of rippling dusks

> My coming is a continent
> Without a frontier,
> The boulder is father of the rock.

Child of the river, child of the rock
child of the rock which lends flying flakes

to pagan winds;
the flakes fashion different legends
in diverse lands:

some spring into domes
some into temples
some into steel-legged pillar
of the bridge in the belly of the river
    some into gold
    some into diamond
    some into multiple stars
    in the firmament of stone

some into castles
some into towers
some into statues which ply their tale
in regions of lenient showers

    some into lyric
    some into song
    some into sculpted flute
    in the hand of whirring winds

some into *gba*
some into *gbu*
some into the *gbaagbuu*
of *Mehunmutapa*

    The boulder is father of the rock
    The boulder is father of the rock
    of sibling slabs lying back to back
    in the family of rooted walls

The boulder is father of the rock.

V

I am child of the river, child of the rock
Child, of rocky hills holding hands
Above the tallest roofs.
Dawns are grey, dusks brown:
Whoever craves the blue legend of Ikere skies,
Let him turn his neck like a barber's chair,
For here the rock is earth, the rock is sky;
Squatters we all on the loamy mercy
Of generous stones

For here the rock is yam
I am child of the river, child of the rock
Of the elephant rock which sleeps
In the eastern sky;
It snores in showers,
The early sun breaks its egg on its sturdy rumps.
I am the yellow yawn of its first hours,
Its red, red nod in hours of homing hues.

I am child of the rock
Too high for the legs of the eye;
For the elephant is feast for any sight
Ah! the elephant is feast;
Whoever takes the jungle's giant
For a passing glance
Craves trampling mortars in his tender farm,
The elephant is feast for any sight

I am child of the rock,
Of the lofty loins of *Ùgèlèmòtirimò**
Who fathers seven broods,
Still seeking the scent of passing maidens.
Oh what ribaldry, the poetry
of romping seasons:

> The okro penis which irks the hungry wife,
> The tireless cunt which swallows a log,
> Still craving a pestle for an itching corner,
> The whistle and baton under the warder's
> baggy shorts,
> The hidden treasure in the school mistress's
> chalk-encrusted skirt

> *Gboó-gbaá labara làbàrà*
> *Gboó-gbaá labara làbàrù*
> Testicle of the ram
> The ewe's feast, the shepherd's pride
> Swinging in the wind
> Swing swing swing swing
> It's swinging in the wind
> *Gbó-gbá labara làbàrà*
> Testicle of the ram

Yours is the season
Of barns let loose in palm oil,
Of *efinrin's*** sniffy courtship of the bride

---

*   One of the huge rocks in Ikere; also associated with Ogunoye fertility songs.
** a plant with mint-like smell whose leaves are used as spice.

Of the nose,
Yours is the stalk which tearfully
Yields its cob to the starving hand,
Pumpkins which roll in the furrows
Like a harvest of juicy raptures.

I am child of *Ùgèlèmòtirimò*
Whose foot is tricky with wet earth
Where wrestling limbs grapple,
And heelmarks echo the wail
Of fallen manhoods.
The season's clay sticks to the memory
Of my toes,
But my back, like the cat's, is clean;
I who leap through the seasons,
Bound to spring, never to lie.

vi

The rock comes to the river
The rock comes to the river
With a limestone smile
And shafts of lofty frowns
The rock comes to the river

In thunder, in lightning
In an August of showers tumbling down
Without warning
Through cobbled pathways
And footfalls of timeless echoes
The rock comes down to the river

The rock takes off its cap of clouds,
Steps out of its dusty slippers
Then bends its hard, hard knees
On the soft mercy of the river bank
The rock dissolves into the river
The river hardens into the rock
Then, the water-buffalo's unseasonal grunt,
The hawing of frogs peeping
Through the grey window of fragile waters

The rock comes to the river
In the rain,
Seven days after the flood which ate
The trees with its copper teeth

    The rock dances
    The river dances

And a boulder touches the river
In its warm, abiding core;
And the river quakes into land
Quakes into sea
Quakes into fire which shapes the fury
Of forging breaths,
Quakes into wind which gives a womb
To wandering seeds ...

    The rock dances
    The river dances

Rockprints on riverloins.

II
What the River said

(Ìbèmbé drums, ṣèkèrè, then the song:
Call! Ẹ jọwọ́ ẹ má ta yẹ̀pẹ̀ si o ⁎
Response: Ẹni ọ̀wọ̀ lẹyẹlééé ...)

i

Child of the rock, child of the river
Child of the river which plies
The world with hidden legs;
Offspring of the mountain
Mother of the rain
Fair of frogs
Roost of happy shoals.
The rock knows the rhythm of swaying water
The rock knows the rhythm of swaying water
Joyful antimony in the eye of the rain-washed paths
The rock knows the rhythm of swaying water

Ẹ`má ta yẹ̀pẹ̀ si o

The river has a song
Oh the river has a song
Pigeon-white, the lyric of the valley
In seasons when lowland floods
Are red with upland clay
And the Maiden, chalk-spotted,
Sways under the compelling benedictions
Of the calabash bowl

⁎   Do not spatter it with mud
    the pigeon is a sacred being
    (The pigeon is Osun's favourite bird)

Ẹ má ta yẹ̀pẹ̀ si o

The river has a song
The river has a song
Deep-timbred tenor of whispering forest,
The raffia suckles its roots,
Its udder springs a lake of honeyed wine.
Bring the keg, bring the gourd
Bring healthy throats so smooth
With the traffic of flowing songs
The pigeon is white, so the wine,
And so this clay from the quarry
Of supple memories
The wine is white
And black, black runs the earth
At the palm's tenacious root
The river has a song

Ẹ má ta yẹ̀pẹ̀ si o

The river has a song
The river has a song
Balm of burning brows
Master of the flame
Murmuring tunnels which wash dawn's face
With a bowl of clouds.
The sky is your depth,
Every boulder bears a womb
Of scarlet flowers

Ẹ má ta yẹ̀pẹ̀ si o

Let me go down with you,
Ageless river,
Behind the trees,
Near the big toe of the hill
Where naked water taunts
The pride of the sponge
And droplets traverse the folds
Their hearts upright like throbbing dreams.
Between sand and water,
In the flower of the water-cress
Which bats the eyelid of waking puddles,
I sound out the shrill of the shell,
My ears pluck the whispers of spotless depths
I walk back home,
My feet chaste like a righteous pledge

    Ẹ má ta yẹ̀pẹ̀ si o

The river has a song
The river has a song
Sun, moon, stars, hills, trees,
The *tiuntiun** which wings its way
Across a blazing noon,
Echoes of the village ballad
Remnants of the city noise
Rumours of the king's fortunes
Tales of the queen's goitre
All so tellingly mirrored
In the palm of the river.

---

* a very small bird with a sharp note

The river is in my eyes
My eyes are in the river
Ah! the river has a song

    Ẹ má ta yẹ̀pẹ̀ si o

I am child of the river
Child of running streams
Which have no harbour for stagnant death
May the season be a pod of many seeds
May the season be a pod of many seeds
The river has a song
The river has a song

The song has a river

    Ẹ má ta yẹ̀pẹ̀ si o

ii

Down the slopes
Down, down the slopes
The flood's red rage,
Fearsome hunger of howling water,
Worsted bridges,
Roads which lost their names,
Walls which melt into mud
Under surprised roofs ...
What liquid energy so current
In its ruthless depths!

The river has a song
In tidings which sweep off
The potsherds of broken seasons
Down down the slope
The river has a song.

iii

The river has a song
The river has a song
In the blossom of affluent banks
Where skybulls swell their rumps,
And lilies wrap the sun in silky petals,
In the vital rot of drifting reed
In the noisy tang of buried shells
The Supple One bleeds every moon to seed
The harvestide;
She who met a world of brown murmurs
Leaving it, seven rains later,
A garden of green songs ...

Soothing, soothing, the melody of the rain
The sky's brief showers which tease the dust
Of the waking day,
The triumphant deluge which pounds the roof
Like incontinent mortars.
Soothing, soothing, the melody of the rain
The fish's squat-legged gallop
*Olúwẹri's** drop-studded crown
In the queendom of the deep
The river has a song

Let swollen lakes count the teeth
Of their crocodiles
Let the hippopotamus bait the wind

---
* water spirit

With a wide, unguarded mouth
Let deserts stretch out their breathless hands

I am a running river
Sundering lands, coupling nations,
Winking here, dimpling there,
Coiling like a patient cobra
Round the foot of towering hills
Deserts stretch out their breathless hands
But my memory charts a path
Of cooler wanderings.

The river has a song

iv

Cascades of pigeons
Cascades of pigeons
A liquid rustle has taken over the sky
Cascades of pigeons
We shall groom next season's bride
In calico and rippling feathers

Cascades of pigeons
Corn-rows on *Olókun's** majestic head;
Ògbèsè** straddles every land,
A wittless flower between her legs,
Oya*** hastens through sand, through loam
To meet her waiting suitors:
Ògún**** lays claim to one breast,
Sàngó+ hangs hot on the other;
Èyékàíre++ sways through iron, through fire
To meet unfolding seasons
Her head a flock of parrot feathers
Her mouth a hatchery of flying visions:

May every vine know a tuber
May every stalk cradle a healthy cob
May their stomach vanish

---

*   Sea-goddess
**   a river, tributary of Osun
***   goddess of the River Niger
**** god of iron
+   god of thunder
++   literally, 'the mother we pet'; another name for Osun priestess at Ile Asa, Ikere

Who want to swallow the earth
May that sword break in its sheath,
Sharpened every morning to behead the world.

V

Cascades of pigeons
Black water pot in the chambers
Of the forest,
Dark darings in wells of indigo waters

And so it was in fresher days
Water called the village, summoned the town,
Then said to the milling crowd:
'Now tell me which of you is my foe'
Water looked left and looked right,
Searched for the poor hardly visible
In their scanty rags,
Then the king whose crown stood so loud
On his greying head
Water looked here, and looked there,
Not one voice rose to counter the soothing one

No dry dirge in the house of the crab,
Freely does the hen strut through
A forest of thorns
Freely.

vi

Cascades of pigeons
Cascades of pigeons
Of the sixteen-flamed lamp burning,
Burning in the universe of the night;
Concourse of moths,
Of the winged termites' brief frolic
In the yellow joy of festive glows

Sixteen-flamed lamp,
Every flame a nail on Ifa's prodigious finger
A care-less sky dips its robe
In the dancing flame,
Then jerks up, its wake a bevy of blazing stars.

Sixteen flames has the lamp
Of She of the Luminous Eyes
In one socket the Sun
In the other the Moon
Which mothers the grove of milky feathers

Fan the flames,
Oh fan the flames
Moon-winged pigeons
Fan the flames,
Yellow-white is the lyric of the wind
Which oils its wick with palms of exuberant groves
When the rain has left
When the flood has swept off the rags
Of tired days
A dove flits across the sky,
A strip of white calico in its beak;

That strip robes the shrubs
And robes the forests
Robes the seasons to their moony bones
Sixteen-flamed lamp
In the season of the rain
The night's loud flicker
Is the colour of the flood,
Of the mortar-bound yam
And corn in deep ferment
And when She steps out
With her luminous eyes
Darkness coils up in swift retreat

Sixteen flames has the lamp
In the ripple of the night;
Clay-laden hands, bead-besotted hips.
The season's yam lies in the upper banks;
Let it reach the door of every mouth
Let it reach the door of every mouth
Let it reach the door of every mouth

vii

Green green green
Green goes my rippling song

Where cornstalks suckle their cradles.
And the millet towers into a tassled sky

The onion's leafy joy sits upon
A stool of redolent marvel

Green green green
Green goes my rippling song

Endless bamboo clumps which oil their rings
With the sweat of loosening plains

Bankfuls of *Òdúndún òkun** whose leaves
Are thrills in melon soups

Green green green
Green goes my rippling song

Àbìrìsókó's** white laughter
Is yellow peril for scooping hoes

Èlú*** carries indigo blood
In its olive veins

---

*   water spinach
** a large, wide-spreading underground tuber which splits the hoe when it is stuck in it.
*** a plant whose leaves are used in dyes.

Green green green
Green goes my rippling song

No dumb earth around my ears
No dumb earth around my ears
I sing in husk, I sing in seed
I sing in flower, I sing in flare
I sing in the moon's own nest, full of eggs
I am a pod of many seeds
I am a pod of many seeds

No dry dirge in the house of the crab
Freely does the hen strut through
A forest of thorns
Freely.

viii

Cascades of pigeons
No one grudges the mouth for its ownership
Of the tongue
No one envies the beard for its loyalty
To the chin
The cap's natural perch is the crest of the head;
Who but She of the Soothing Hand
Can slay this thirst in the throat of the world?

>The well of goodness never dries
>The well of goodness never dries
>No dry dirge in the house of the crab
>Freely does the hen strut through
>A forest of thorns
>Freely.

ix

I am light
I am shadow
I am the luminous covenant
Of short and tall spaces

I am child of the rock, child of the river
Mid-day river which mirrors the prancing sun

      I
am caller at noon.

III
Human in every sense

I am caller at noon
the hole of that key
the key of that door
the door of that house
the house of that street
the street of that town
the town of that country
the country of that world
where rooms are large
and a smiling yam whispers yes
to every hunger;
I am also the hinge of eternal windows,
the spine of the book of life.
So when you walk, never bruise your shadow:
I am the pearl of your laughter,
the watering passion of your garden of tears

I am the speck of dust in the evening air
bubbling butterfly in the estate of the flower,
kite in a mellow sky,
foe of the storm, friend of the wind,
if I come near your mirror
I am instantly a lavender of eternal fragrance
if I settle near your garden
I am loam of immeasurable promise;
touch me with the dew of a generous dawn
and I turn talkative clay in your moulding hands.
I am cactus, veteran of stubborn mercies,
mining fluent chatter from the accent
of ancient sands,

porcupine though my masks,
my limbs a patient tablet of pilgrim scrawls:
polyglot my joy, my tattoos desperate vows
of fleeting lovers.

I am the forest of the desert
the stem of every sand, branch of every speck,
giant moss on the brow of the dune,
amazingly green;
I am the wind which sculpts the sand
into magnificent patterns
I am the bridle of the sandstorm: I steer
the sirocco's savage horse from tracks
of wanton ruin.

I look through the sand, I see a fountain,
I look through the fountain, I see the river
I look through the river, I see the sea
I look through the sea, I see the sky.
I am the bard who sings of water
in shrivelled seasons.
I say to the oasis: why don't you swell
and swallow the desert?
I tell the desert: why don't you let the rain ...?
There is something celestial, I say,
in the moistening lips of pubescent showers

I trace the way of the camel and ponder
the endless patience of the beast's ungainly hump
I ask its long legs, I ask its narrow eyes
I ask the invisible cistern in the kitchen
of its throat;
I ask the Tuareg's wizened beard,

footprints of old terrors when salt swapped
hands for pepper, then for teeming lives
from Africa's beleaguered forests.
The Tuareg casts a glance,
and a scroll of chronicles rolls down his silent face;
I chase those chronicles to a distant coast,
the Mediterranean springs a mask
of dated sages.
I have been through the desert
but there are no sands in the ointment
of my mind

My gold comes from the quarry of the setting sun
my silver from the joyous fin of the sea's abiding tribes
the hen's fresh-laid eggs are the cornea
of my eyes
my body harbours a river in every vein:
the Euphrates, the Ganges, the Mississippi,
the Volga, the Rio, the Niger all seek a shore
in the confluence of my heart;
my fire comes from the parrot's enflamed tail
my camwood from àlòkò's* red fable;
the sky is my robe
the sky is my robe
my cottonfields are up in the clouds
the sky is my robe

I am what is, is not
the fiction of the fact

---

*   bird with a deep-red colour

the fact of impossible fictions
I am the tail which leads the head
the mouse which worsts the league
of a thousand cats
I am the watering eyes of a savannah
tormented by dubious fires,
I am the mahogany's last curse
on the greedy axe;
I am the grain which blooms the valley
after a handsome shower,
the coquettish lash on the eye of green cliffs.
I am earth's twilight yawn
and also her vigilant dawn:
When I die, Earth will throw open her bosom,
let gravediggers spare their morbid axe.

I am human in every sense
lover of life without regret
ample hips, the bouncing bosom
handsome lips alive with joy
tongues which twist and tangle like exultant vines
a tickle in the armpit, a tickle in the groin
the cool-hot hearth in the valley of the legs
the pestle finds its mortar
the mortar finds its pestle
legs touching legs in a dance beyond the drum
a gentle sigh, a sticky moan
hard and soft is the legend of the flame.
I have seen eyes more eloquent
than a hundred tongues:
the beckoning brow, the warrant of the wink;

I have plucked furtive glances like
a precocious orange,
read a thousand chapters in the book
of the whisper
plunged down, down the depth of the smile

I hold life like a brimming cup
vinegar at times, for the most, wine
with irrepressible spirits.
I drink in song, I drink in dance
I drink, but not too far below the brim:
when I pick my share, I leave the garden behind.

The head leads, the heart follows
The heart leads, the head follows
I think to love, I love to think,
I wear no masks of craven virtues,
for my heart once said to me:
'Be not ashamed of me'.

The pine-apple left its honey in my mouth,
the loam-fattened yam put a bounce on my biceps,
*tòlótòló's** thigh is drumstick in my simmering soup;
I share the guinea-corn's glory in the furnace
of the sun,
I trace the way of the grape,
the juicy tang of sleeping cellars,
palm-wine's frothy rage in the divinity of the gourd,

---

*   turkey

and redolent vows yeasting, yeasting
in the calabash of fleeting seasons.

Let all who sow
share in the harvestfeast
Let all who sow
Share.
The pot which cooks the season's delicacies
must cool its scorched bottom
with the tastiest of royal banquets
Let all who sow
Share.

I hold life like a brimming cup
vinegar at times, for the most, wine
with irrepressible spirits.
I sing a calf to every cow,
to every pig a barn of noisy sows.
I am spirit of the streamside:
my eyebrows are shrubs, incessantly green.

I sing the plenitude of being.

My memories mould the pyramids,
unsilence the Sphinx
rinse pagan hieroglyphs in the Nile
arrest the crack of Pharoah's whip.
I am a lamp in the tunnel, bold and bright,
beacon in the blindness of the night,
beckoning ships ashore from the wildness

of the sea.
I am the spirit of the making mind
at war with brittle facts
at war with groggy superstitions statued
into giants with iron legs
at war with wills which say yes
to the blood-stained accent of unmanning edicts
at war with spirits afraid of thinking
at war with those who murder the world
with the myth of jealous gods
at war with the hectoring jab, with canons
which whip the world into a hard, invariate mould
at war with former victims of fire who thrive now
through the commerce of the gun
at war with the crocodile who swallows the minnows
at war with all who hasten the day
towards a sudden twilight ...
For when life's breathing fingers knock on the door,
I am always there, waiting behind the knob.

I am friend of the eye which looks and sees
explorer of mass, prober of matter
of the several squares which mother the circle
the ripen physics of the falling apple
the chilling temper of the furnace
the blinding heat of ice
the instructive energy of a bird in flight
the part which outweighs the whole
the leaden albatross of the atom ...
The knowing mind is the eye of the body
with no truant pupils and catarracts
of waterless brows.

Oh what have I done, people of our land,
what have I done?
I haven't taken the doe from her handsome deer
I haven't grudged the ram for its frightful horns
I haven't pinched a kobo from the usurer's tormenting purse
I haven't envied the eye as the bird of the face

For if speed were a function of legs
the millipede would have no rival
in the race of the forest;
if wisdom were a direct offspring of the magnitude
of the head,
no beast would challenge the buffalo
in the discourse of the grassland;
if cunning could bestow a towering height
the snake would be the hissing Kilimanjaro
of the shrub.

Were the rich man to have his way
the world would be a vault of gold,
were *amúnisìn** to heed one half of his wish
the universe would be a fortress of slaves
were *Kénimánî*** a god with infinite powers
the earth would beg for one grain of corn.
We say the hyena is now lord of the wilds
We say the hyena is now lord of the wilds
Whosoever still seeks peace in the fold of hapless duikers?

---

*   slave maker
** ill wisher

Verily, verily as the ewe is wife of the ram
I am the caller at noon,
the breeze which stirs your eaves
in the shadow of the softening rain.
I am every thing, I am no thing,
the tail which drives flies for the helpless bull
the nose which leads the head in a peak
of redolent seasons.
I am the slave who drudges at the feast
and starves on crumbs
I am the mason who hews stones
and pines in a muddy shack
I am the peasant in whose palms
the matchet forgot its handle
I am the miner lost to light in the joyless abyss
of diamond magnates
I am a cockroach trapped in the brimming sewage
of opulent cities
I am a rolling whisper in a wilderness of voices
I am an echo lost among the hills.

I know all this
I know it all
For I was there when the hawk swooped at dusk
and the hen's joys disappeared between its claws
I was there when *àrògidìgbà** heaved open its funeral jaws
and a tribe of minnows became a tale

---

* a large, greedy fish

I was there
child of the rock, child of the river
farmer's son, scion of the hoe
servant of the forest, but also its master.
I have felt the needling pinch of the morning dew,
the harmattan's sandy swoop
and the sun which burns like a greedy furnace
in the hearth of Ẹgbàkè* sky.
I have known the land, the land has known me
I have reaped merciless dust in epochs
of long droughts, sat down to hunger,
and suffered endless nights on a mat
severely lean with winkless straw.
I have seen locusts black out the sun
before settling down to a harvest of funeral leaves
I have seen teeming households thinned
down to an orphan by a convoy of avoidable plagues
I have seen the sword dancing, dancing
through the column of plebeian necks

I have seen all this and more
And I can never forget.

'Sing us a happy song, oh poet!.
I hear mild protestations from the edge
of the crowd,

---

*   meaning top of the hill; where the poet's father had his farm.

'Sing us sunny songs, joyous like the showers
of April,
crisp like a piece of *ewùrà** placed white-hot
on the plate of the smiling child.
Sing to us about rivers, rivers tumbling
down the mountains with a concert
of chorusing fishes.
Sing to us about hills galloping against the sky
like a happy rig of *Udi*** horses
Sing to us about egrets echeloned
in the Christmas sky,
a chalky epigram of infinite spaces
Sing to us about the antelope which brightens
the forest with its handsome leaps
Sing to us about paths which meet and part,
part and meet in wandering jungles
Sing to us about the glow-worm's treason
in the darkdom of night

Sing to us about Soyinka, Guillèn, Brathwaite,
Neto, Walcott, Ai Qing, Heaney, Mayakovsky,
Okigbo, U Tamsi, Okot p' Bitek;
about Neruda, bard of Chile, father of songs,
About Whitman who wrapped the world
in leaves of eloquet grass

Sing to us about Elytis' small world the great,
Vallejo's big-hatted verse,

---

* water yam
** a mountain range in the eastern part of Nigeria

the laughing lemons of Darwish, victim of a map,
who turned friend of the corn
the day his poems were made of earth
where the feet of the mountain drink the sea;
and Adonis who sailed in the Ark,
reaching liquid skies through the window of prayers

Sing to us about Huidobro,
about the magic lyre of Octavio Paz,
Zapata's arrow in the bow of flying ballads;
about Czeslaw Milosz, 'child of Europe',
walking through the malignant wisdom
of broken cities,
about Amiri Baraka who gathers briefs cinders
for coming thunders,
about Rabindranath Tagore who plants marble lines
on the brow of the Taj Mahal;
about Aime Cesaire whose fear squats
in purple streets, in bardic quest
for a tree with a thousand roots

Sing to us about bards, troubadors, griots, towncriers
who joined the earth but left their voices behind.

Sing to us about
the mouth which finds its tongue
the face which finds its nose
the pen which finds its nib
the groom who meets his bride
the slave who breaks his chains ...
Sing to us about all this
Sing all this, o poet, and more!'

I am the triumphant sheen of the sickle
in the sun of the harvestide
I am the grain which tumbles into the barn,
a golden chatter on every lip
I am the yam dug out of the mound,
swathed in earth's prodigious fragrance
I am the prolific vulva of the melon,
corncobs which drape their spines
with a den of healthy teeth
I am denizen of the forest
I know the secret whisper of courting trees.

When I woke up this morning, the stone was
on the podium;
its sermon was harsh, its vision a gritty apocalypse
of crashing boulders.
The scorpion scribbled a joke on a wondering slab;
reading it, the spider broke into a web
of rippling laughter;
the lizard saw it all, its head a restless
chapter of philosophic nods:
always on all fours, always on its belly,
passing moons have no cure for its aching guts.
The stone spoke its sermon, the morning wondered,
but *Olosunta**
looked on in lofty bemusement:
> Who gave these pebbles the prophesy of a tongue;
> Who gave mere outcrops the vision of settled rocks?

---

* Father of Rocks: the most imposing rockhill in Ikere

*Èèwòọ!** a mere loinstrip has usurped
the glory of the robe,
errant chips lay claim to the splendour of the quarry.
Season of straw masks, season of noisy tales
season of straw masks waiting for the baptism
of the torch.
Everywhere lakes rub waters with the sea,
the rabbit parodies the gait of the buffalo,
the sword outgrows its sheath, wondering
down the warrior's hips ...
Who gave you stone the power of augury?
Boulders indeed will fall. But why can't
you see those bleeding statues
which will litter their wake;
why don't you mention castles
with rioting slabs,
then the crimson gaze of wounded crowns
How didn't you see falling boulders
magnifying into rockheads below the hill,
on the grassless beach, beating back
the sea's rapacious sharks coming,
all ways coming, a century of chains
hidden behind their scurvy grins?

Preach us sermons about thickening nights,
but sing songs also about the breaking day.
For the night is a rapid stop
between two suns,

---

*   Taboo!

sure as every branch is a journey
towards its leaves

Between song, between dance,
in ready answer to *àgbá's** majestic throb,
Olósunta spoke, *Òròólẹ̀*** nodded
Ẹ̀sìdálẹ̀*** rattled his ancient knuckles,
the skies rumbled, the rain descended
earth cradled a new yam
in every hearth.

Every god is man
every man is god:
the Cross the Crescent, the squatting Budha —
all monuments of our ancient fears.
Every god is man
with his own jealous tantrums
holy pogroms and martyrs of fugitive faith.
I ask Ọbàtálá again:
who moulded the mountain on the hunchback,
the albino with darting eyes;
I ask Ògún how forge-red iron sizzles
when provoked by the gore of prodigal battles.
Who will tell Sàngó
to his kola-eyed face:

---

* a man-size drum beaten during Olosunta festival
** pyramid-shaped rock in Ikere
*** founder, earth-creator

it is true indeed you hanged at Kòso?
Every god is man
every man is god.
The gods someday must die
that man himself may live ...

Sirens, buntings, and billowing banners
Sirens, bugles and rolling cannon.
And enter Hitler with the burning bush
of his shifty moustache
Enter Bokassa with infant skulls
in his imperial pot.
Enter Pinochet with Allende's blood on his iron bow
Enter Botha, Biko's brain under his spiked boot
Enter the Iron Lady with five testicles like a Juba squirrel
Enter the Horseman, a sanguinary twilight
in his rigid gaze
And the world going round, round, and round
like a giddy mask

Empires rise, decline, and fall,
from their ashes, new juggernauts and new swords
and conquistadors who sail the skies
with vassals on every coast,
marching through tender dreams,
pillaging distant lands to prosper their own.
And round and round and round
the Sword raises its sunset song,
I vision a world which says No
to the dirge of coffin-makers.

This morning I saw a tree weeping
at the edge of a smouldering forest,
its branches bruised, its roots sad like carrots
withering on the market tray.
I asked the matchet
I asked the saw
I asked the bulldozer which brutes the wilds
in bovine fury,
I asked the timber-magnate waiting at the port,
a blue greed in his eyes
I saw the proud *ìrókò*, once tree, now log,
lying without a name.

I took off my clothes by the long-accustomed lake,
and a dying fish showed me the silent fire
in its limpid water.
The sea now tomb for lethal salts,
where will the salmon spawn eternal summers?
Unnatural gales rip off the roof of the sky,
the moon staggers into night, a dark tear
in each eye.
Where is he, where is he?
Where is the vandal who punched a hole
in the garment of our sky?
Now every rain is a storm
the sun is ready fire above our broiling heads ...

And yet I am the brittle tale
on the lips of budding branches
the yellow petal which heralds the green majesty
of the teeming pod,
I am the awesome canopy of the rain forest
the silent seed roused to song

by the Monsoon's uncluttered breath
The deer lends me his horn
the antelope loans me the grace of her legs
the kangaroo shelters galloping seasons
in its masurpial pouch,
I am the measured amble of the caterpillar,
the transfiguring luminescence of the chameleon
I am every thing
I am no thing.
So when you stab the wondering tree
I am the one that bleeds.

'See with your whole body', my mother said,
'your whole body'
'See with your whole body', that is what
the bush fowl told its fledgeling brood.
'Hunters are cunning, the gun is fast,
the bullet tastes ash in the chambers
of a dying jaw.
Your sauce is sweet,
a thousand mouths water for the hunter's return
See with your body;
the bush fowl's body is eyes, feathers and all.
A sharp-visioned mind is the laughter
of the fowl'.

'See with your body', said she,
her voice assured, her face open like a book.
Some spy the mask, swearing they have
seen the face,
some see the cloud and vow it is the sky
some marvel at the river oblivious of its depth.

The snake hides its legs only from the hasty eye
the hen's teeth are deep in its hardy stomach.
What secret has the fire, ask the silent ash
what secret has the toe, ask the dust
He who listens with all ears
will hear the footsteps of ants

'See with your body
What mystery drives the cow to the butcher's table
ask its hump,
what thunder riles the throat of the barking dog
ask its sturdy teeth
what marvel makes Ifa the cradle of wisdom
ask tooth-eyed cowries of the divining tray

'See with your body
Have you ever pondered the stab behind the smile
the mirth behind the myth
the dog behind the god?

'See with your body
Ponder the silence of the noise,
the noise of every silence
the bitterness of honey
the lacerating coldness of the sun
Ponder the thirty-year old pounded yam
which still burns the flippant finger
'See with your body
Then count the legs of the millipede
the porcupine's quills
the stars of a cloudless sky.
Count how many drops make up the sprawling sea

'See with your body
For when cutting a tree, it is only the wise
who watch out for the destination of the leaves,
when others rouse the dragon, it is the thoughtful
who measure the strength of the village fist,
when they provoke a deluge, it is the shrewd
who mind the sinews of the roof

'See with your body
For life's millipede is more than the sum
of its legs,
the thunder of living is louder than
what the ear remembers,
When the world grips you in dialogue,
watch its lips
but
tilt your ears to its puzzling mind.

See with your body
For knowledge is not wisdom
mere cleverness can never be a peer of infinite nous;
a thousand books may not total one strand
of the beard of a quiet proverb.
Look deep, my child
Deep, deep does Earth hide her countless gems
Deep, deep does the rodent burrow
in the breast of the hill
Deep, deep does the tree hide its venturing roots
Deep, deep ...

I am every thing
I am no thing
I rise from a bench in a public park,
but the bench holds on to a fragment of me;
I look closely at the pensive river,
and the river saunters downhill
with my wondering eye;
I whisper a tune between the hills
and my voice bursts out into golden echoes

I am every thing
I am no thing
when I shake hands with a positive spirit
a blue spark ignites my mind
when I meet the starved and acutely rattled
my stomach turns a house of hunger;
when I hear groans of the heavy-laden
my heart sprouts a million fists;
when I walk through the fire of battle
my shadow takes up a thousand shields

I am every thing
I am no thing
When the day departs,
it leaves the sun at my door;
when the night goes to sleep,
the moon nestles in the bosom of my dream
when I go to the lake to bathe,
the surrounding shrub is a fair of fragrant soap.
I am every thing
I am no thing

Give me the power to send words on errands
launch capsuled proverbs like fire-tailed rockets,
tinge every idiom's arrowpoint with hues
of furnaced gold.
My memory is a hieroglyph of untold tales,
striving, like crabs, striving for a hold
in the bottom of a slippery pail,
reaching for air, reaching for space.
The valley is deep,
the mountaintop giraffe-high.
Oh give me wings, you waters of blue shadows,
speed me with your feathered sandals,
robe me in your gossamer breath,
skybound like an eagle so sure
of the competence of the wind.
Syllables sweat in the forge of the larynx,
lines sprawl out their frames like basking pythons
adjectives find their nouns, verbs their active shadows
every stanza is a night waiting for a breaking day.
When I split the kola of wisdom
let every lobe fall face-up like a sunny pledge

Lend me ears for the whisper of the wind
the breath of the forge
the clay's destiny in the pit of the moulding palm
Give me the power to send words on errands
tell reticent stars their hidden names,
give thunder's accent to the murmur of the moon,
a tongue to passing seasons,
root to waiting laughters.
The world bestrides my dreams like a giant car;
my tongue seeks the certainty of the word.
When I split the kola of wisdom

let every lobe possess a sunny heart

Give me power to send words on errands
Give me words beyond words.

Omi l'ènìà ...... Humanity is a river
Omi l'ènìà .... Humanity is a river
Tó bá ṣàn wá .... When it flows forth
A tún ṣàn padà ..... It also flows back
Omi l'ènìà .... Humanity is a river

Those who passed have not parted
Those who passed have not parted
Their footprints settle the crest of every wave
Their mindprints thrive the leaves of fire
Which brighten the step of every word

Those who passed have not parted
They are the song in the hills
echoes which winnow the idiom of gathering caves,
the boulder down the slope, wisely smooth
from every toss ...
They are the roots whose hands confirm the tree,
the wind whose breath compels the leaves.
Those who passed have not parted:
the pounded yam of a thousand years
still burns the itching finger.
Those who passed have not parted:
They are the fragrant armpit of the seasons
April's prickly showers,
the redolent carpet of the rain forest

the piquant bite of the Sahara wind ...
Omi l'ènià

A long, wide river we all are
gentle here, ferocious there,
freezing here, and there hot like molten bronze,
some seething with crocodiles of macabre fury,
others eloquent with untainted minnows ...
But together we chase the waiting sea
Together we chase the waiting sea
The waiting sea
Together we chase the waiting sea
Together ...

Omi l'ènià

If we do not meet in the rapid mountains
we strike a tryst in the gentle plains

Omi l'ènià

The star finds its name in the galaxy of night
the fish spells its face in the book of fugitive shoals.
The snake which roams the wild in the company
of its skin
soon finds its head under the hunter's club.
Pebbles which join heads will form a rock,
trees which share branches will form a forest.
What name do we call it, that hand
whose tribe is memory of a sole finger?
Omi l'ènià

One broomstick cannot sweep the street
One broomstick cannot sweep the street
Our memory is a cluttered traffic of sordid litterings
One broomstick cannot sweep the street

Omi l'ènià

And the Mississippi joins the Niger
in a many-fingered pledge before the sea;
the Zambezi greets the Yukon in dialects
of icy mountains;
the Nile is one long smile awaiting the grape —
draped embrace of the Rhine;
the Thames serenades the Ganges festooned
on saddles of nodding elephants;
the Paraña's laughter is wheat and wandering wool

Omi l'ènià

My yam grows in the Pampas,
my cassava in the prairies;
a tribe of wheat sinks its immigrant root
in the rolling welcome of my tropical savannah.
My hoe speaks the language of the sky:
I farm the world

Omi l'ènià

I am the ubiquitous *and* in the broken
scene-tax of a stammering discourse,
the *but* which tempers the flame
of volcanic clauses;
I am the pronoun, loyal envoy of

an ambiguously substantive past;
I am the period, the stick's last tap
on the countenance of the drum.

Omi l'ènìa

'Sing us another song!'
I hear an impatient rustle in the garment
of the crowd,
another song, oh poet,
for the moon of our throat is high
in the sky of the drum,
our corn of laughter craves immediate plucking

* * *

Shall I tell you then
about the foolish man
who died on a rainy day
and shouted to the world, "Can't you see,
even God is weeping my death?"

* * *

Or that pretentious man
whose rags raised laughing dust in every street,
when asked: why so many holes in your garb,
he said they were mere windows
in the house of his body

***

People of our land,
Pity the plight of my stomach:
I have not tasted pounded yam
for several seasons,
now my morsels come thin and tiny —
like the coconuts of Badagry!

***

Jombele jòmbè jòmbè jòmbè
Jombele jòmbè jòm
My story has legs ...

Sàgbàyìgí wanted to see his image
framed up and hanged in one corner
of his tinbox room.
He once saw his face
in a mirror in the chief's house
and he liked what he saw ...

So *Sàgbàyìgí* raked up his fortune
and off he went to the photographer's shop.
"Agiripa Photos" rolled out his kit,
mounted the magic box,
fussed forward, fussed backward,
and was just about to pull the shutter
when an inexplicable wonder froze his hand:

The man who posed before him
had left his face at home!

Jombele jòmbè jòmbè
My story has legs
but it will not run away

* * *

Who still asks why Jambute is thin?
he eats, standing behind the wall,
the food forsakes his stomach
going straight into his twitching calves

* * *

And this short tale
about Ubiye's goat:
Ubiye is blind in the right eye,
her goat in the left;
tell me, if the goat steals your yam,
how can you curse a one-eyed thief
without offending its equally afflicted owner? ...

Give me the power to send words on errands
Give me the power ...
My song is a mansion with a million rooms,
many-petalled flower, hills of countless echoes,
the gentle stream which stumbles into song
on the rounded rock of noon.
The rainbow's pride is a garment of many colours
The rainbow's pride is a garment of many colours
My song is a mansion with a million rooms

I am human in every sense
the tree-lined wonder of the Amazon,
the wheat-tinged beard of the Aconcagua;
the *Kùkùrùkù* croons in the shadows of my sun.
Continent without frontiers,
I am a caller at noon.

IV
Breaking walls

I am every thing
I am no thing

And the early sun plying shy fingers through
the green-yellow turf of September's forest

And the wind, talkative, still, on a flute
breathed to life from a tornado's ruins

And the squirrel losing tail and nut to a seductive breeze,
erect like a cave-ward shaft

And the blunted blades of the leaves,
gallant stalks whispering mortal pleas

    To the wind's empowered summon

And the trees sloughing their fears, dreaming
new skins for the season's unmerciful coming

And a husky speck unsettles the wind, rust-tempered,
memory of a harvest that was

And young women with handsome thighs compound
ambitious gazes with the regal stride of practiced mermaids

And the river unravels its tongue between the trees'
rooted sentry and a clan of wild grass

And ducks which unsilence its face, a giant screen
with cryptograms of unhideable ripples

And the mower, dancing through the pubic jungle
of the lawn, its teeth green with hymeneal complaint

And the men who move the mowers, their pulsating biceps,
their breaths heavy with subjugated fragrance

And shadows which chase their substance,
at the fleeting mercy of a distant sun

And children romping to school the sky in their eyes,
at their feet, crossroads of a thousand dreams

And the rainbow which unwinds the sky,
arched like an unforgivable laughter.

Breaking walls, walls breaking
in the chilly summon of the dungeon
where silence rides the crest of purple groans
and murmurs pluck their wails from
    the testimony of ruptured spleens

Breaking walls
in the spiked stammer of iron heels polished
to blinding shimmer in a lake of steaming blood,
laced to frenzy by the dripping tendons
    of rifled joints

An iron knuckle unsettles the martial peace of the door
hinges surrender their teeth, and a gecko falls
from the splice of the chaos, flat, medievally dry;
peepholes are blind in one eye; the knob stiffens,
    convulsed beyond recall

Mosquitoes brook the rap without a wink,
serenading indulgently between their meals;
the cockroach preens its pride above the door,
its coat a faithful mirror for blind batons
    aloft on shaven skulls

No sun here: the sky is once upon a season:
a window interrupts the eternity of the wall,
unspaced by iron bars, too high to see the moon;
the sky is a wilderness of barbed wire, of broken bottles
    still sad for their wasted wine.

A guard grabs Detainee 13130013 by the arm,
his skin comes off in scarbrous ease;
another prisoner coughs in Cell 770077,
the yard a swarming compost
    of tubercular plague

Music here comes in symphonies of swinging whips
the rasp of iron knuckles on the harp of baring ribs
the tom-tom of the truncheon on the base of stubborn spines
sirens of passing powers, rat-a-tat
    of brainless coups

    And enter the generals
    in crunching boots
    and monologues
    of talkative triggers

    Their whiskers are iron
    their lips stone slabs
    of crimson edicts;
    their gait is gore, stairs

Creak under their breaths;
Sandhurst in their lungs
empire in their dreams
their master's voice so

Loud above their clashing cymbals;
they sentry the exit of wit
shout out the light from
the lamps of venturing feet

Bendless their joints,
kneading ash from breathing clay
plodding across the land, gun —
prints of shells and spent virtue

Fat and rich
they shoot blind guns at tender fortunes,
retire into billions at thirty years,
pampered emperors on purchased thrones

Says Galileo: the earth I see is round.
And Lorca's head comes smiling in Franco's platter
And Defoe's plague years, within the Crown's slit
in his dissenting ears
And Paine's countless wrongs for tomorrow's rights
And Brecht hit the waves, Hitler's headhunters
on his epic heels

Says Galileo: the earth I see is round

And Brutus's ballad, and the Apartheid dragon
And Soyinka's shuttle in the General's crypt
And Ngugi's travails on the Devil's cross
And Mapanje's chameleons and Band – it gods

Says Galileo: the earth I see is round

Then come jagged visions flat as a foil, saracens of lame scriptures, sooth-murderers purple in tooth and claw, peddlers of expired faiths, bile merchants, book-burners, maulers of the breathing word, night moles, fabricators of monochromatic rainbows, scarlet prowlers, knights of the smoking gun

And waiting noons are twilights of pounding hooves, of crimson dust which falls back to earth, a tribe of sprawling corpses; and the bridle sews the jaws of the horse: galloping days are bedlam of neighing tantrums; and iron trots break the spine of the streets; houses look on with dusty eyes, their eaves dropping like tired ears; and warriors thunder down the roads, a cavalry of broken vows.

And streamward maidens lose their flowers, and homeward hunters forgo their game, and ripening farms forget the barn, and harvest seasons escape their laughter, and they swallow the mountain, wash it down with the happiest lake, then sew up the sky into *boubous* of infinite pockets

And the sky invokes its thunder, and thunder invokes its lightning: and the *boubou* blooms into a pageant of fire, and their ashes nurture the waiting loam.

Dare you who will. Dare you, deans of universal nescience. Dare you conquer truth with bayonets and cannon; your legs are two, but there are many crossroads on the pilgrimage to enduring wisdom.

Says Galileo: the earth I see is round

So, has Socrates brewed his hemlock? Tell this to the vanishing sun, you who stand between the bee and its hive, the hen and its lay, the parrot and its tale, the weaverbird and its nest.
Tell it to the bushfowl which turns a night of envy when the egret drapes the sky in chalky splendour, the *gànyinganyin** which grudges the pine-apple for its house of honey, the snail which dreams daggers for the antelope's savannah heels.

Tell this to the waking sun: this hemlock courts the pride of the emperor's lips – our dawn has no more nails for the cross of unsinning Christs.

Breaking walls
which block the house from the festival of the street

Breaking walls
which part the mouth from the prayers of the ear

Breaking walls
which steel the heart against the touching hand

---

*   very sour orange

Breaking walls
which seal the desert from the plea of the rain

Breaking walls
which deaden the night to the whisper of the dew

Breaking walls
sowing fertile tears in the laughter of stone
laying quiet mines for the swagger of steel

Breaking walls
levelling the fence, un-ironing the Curtain
driving idle clouds off the face of the sun

Breaking walls
into a universe of doors
pasture of acute windows

Breaking walls
for the door is the eye of the wall
the window its spacious ear

V
Diary of the Sun

<u>a</u>

Have I offended the sun
Have I offended the sky
Have I trampled one shred
of the day's voluminous robe?

Have I offended the sea
Have I offended the river
Have I spilled one drop
of the lake's unmeasurable water?

These eyes have seen beaks
These eyes have seen feathers
These eyes have seen *yeyerémò**
Chirruping across the sky of the moon

These eyes have counted
the egret's ivory blessings
on the nails of chanting children;
these days have seen kitchen smokes

Twirl skywards for a feast in the clouds;
our palm-oil cannot sleep under the gaze
of a fiery noon: a red honour
unpales the humour of our soup.

A heady sun disbands the army
of solider-ants: mortar heads

---

*   a flock of tiny, high-flying birds, common in dry season twilights in Southern Nigeria.

scramble into the bunker of fright.
Lying shadows are rare faces

    In
the commerce of our noon

b

And the sun combing the tree's temple
like a spotlight finding its quarry
on a wide and crowded stage ...

My acts are many,
uncountable scenes lurk behind the winds
dark aisles are white with the prompting energy

of waiting laughters. The sky this time an orchard
of ripening suns, red with rage, black with hope,
white with exquisite peace of coming egrets:

the cyclorama of my spine is a harvest
of athletic moods, galloping upstage like thoroughbreds,
inching up the orchestra pit like a sonorous snail.

Stage-centre stand I, brow a glistening calendar.
of passing seasons, on my breast garlands of moon maidens;
in my hand a sword which left its sheath in thunder's house

Midlife's masks are gossamer from the chisel of the sun
lengthening feet untangle the steps hurriedly taken
in dawns of exuberant mists.

c

The sun midscene in the sky's diurnal drama
skyroutes pebbled like a quarry,
some cold and sharp against the journeying sole,
others smooth and sagely like remnants of ancient rocks.

And the large bright dreamway
narrowing here, widening there,
pilgrimmed with stubborn visions of sinewy throngs
dreamsides tough with limbless whimpers

Of executed bones. Few called, many chosen.
In the unleavened wilderness of tempted passions,
frocked visions select their eyes, the bell
garners ears like a corn-sickle.

There is a swollen pestilence at the root of the
Word:
husbandsmen have drowned in the ocean
of the flesh; poison weeds bloom and brag

like tendrils of lying rains

Midscene, sift-time for tares of noonsome harvests.

d

And a rapid bird taxes down the runway
of waiting trees, its webbed landing slippery
on leaves emulsified by the sun;
frightened stalks carry the tale to the busy branches

Which nod and smile like intrepid sages.
They have seen leaves come and go
like fancy garments in the wardrobe of seasons;
but the rain has a door that drought's

fiery breath cannot open.

In nearby fields the hoe tickles the humus,
redolent high noons when rotting roots
pledge the bloom of the barn,
and the grasshopper's yellow corpse awaits

the green hearse of April's unsure shower.

The dibble knows its job, finding growing homes
for grains long stranded in the streets of the cob.
The moon promises a rasping duel
when green swords bloom the loin of tranquil stalks

and bumblebees bass their way through
a happy mesh of pollen grains.
Distant yet the dialect of the sickle:
grey the tassel in the ear of the sun

e

I leave footprints in the dust,
brown, singing songs of red tidings

The elephant heaves past its unwieldy limbs
but my echo survives its trampling trunk

The jackal sneaks past its funeral stomach
its jaws still locked in tragic laughter

I leave footprints in the dust
the tornado calls, the tempest responds

But a thousand gales cannot
shift the memory of my sole.

And nomads find a mirror for the camel
of their truth, humped with pride

Humped with promise; humped with rain
in a dialogue of droughts

A map, oh a map with veils and veins:
toemarks of delta in a sea of sands.

The heel is a mountain with a tender peak,
midsole a valley of tickling shrubs

I leave footprints in the dust
bright with shadows, quick with words

Every line a curve of the alphabet of the sun

f

White-hot with wisdom
the sun lends a wild name
to the tame anonymities
    of cold and mysty dawns

Brows now find their place
in the sharp-visioned cliff
above the eye, lips encounter
    solid geometries in the labial chatter.

Between the jaws. A solar patience
unmasks the crowd, counting vital tremors
in the volcanic shibboleth
    of impatient noses.

The sun's eyes are eagle,
picking tiny scars —
a camera raking wounded flocks
    for the bleeding saga of unsinning tails.

Red noon. The circumcising sun
hangs between the sky,
deliberate, cruelly kind
    Ah! a grey-hot edge has fine —

Ally breached the prepuce of the mist:
the day knows now the dialect
of the knife. I throw red-ringed shouts
    at the hills of the sky

Skyvalleys will return my voice
when the sun's riddling knife has know
its sheath, and twilight wears its scars
    like a fertile-garland.

My wound is a map
with bleeding rivers

and lakes of accumulated sweat;
my biceps are mountains

plundered through history
of the treasury of their bronze.

moons join hands with stars,
but they cannot circle the comp —

ass of the scar;
the conquistador's whip

exacts its latitude
on ebony backs hunched

like swindled hills;
unequal longitudes run the equinox

of our noons where forests,
pygmy in the towering chronicle

of fable makers,
mould new branches towards the sun.

h

(Goshen, Indiana)

And the sun traces the geo
graphy of History on my glistening brow:
tell-tale creases, rippling like water snakes
into the dense foliage of the head

The nose is a heaving island
in the ocean of the face
redolent (still) with vanished whimpers
and the tropical memory of unborn seasons

In the valley between my lips
legends sprout like mushrooms in the first rain,
with domes of fire,
caryatids of eloquent bronze.

There are hungry tremors
in the mountains of the jaw:
a drought-tested spittle slobbers down
the cliff of the palate, the tong

ue is one pink fire in the furnace
of the mouth, slicing through mosaics
of muted murmurs, through dark threnodies
of manacled spurs.

These ebony contours in the deciduous interludes
of evergreen joys, counting pits and peaks
in the solar tempers of undulating masks.
The sun knows the geo-graphy of History.

i

(for Mary, for Valley Avenue)

And with your mouth minted with jasmine
of the riverside, plucked when earth's grace
is green with the grandeur of affectionate rains

Your fingers quick, still, with the fable
of the sap, your eyes bright petals
so full of the legend of the lake,

You saunter down the valley of noon,
earth is your sole, the sky
your crown of unmatchable blue.

Tender as a wink, seraphically true,
you scatter sunny sagas in the loam
of lingering noons, distant shadows

Are orchards of ripening laughters

i

    under the trees
    where shadows pick
    their dark teeth

with shovels straight   sprouting tongues gather
from the sun's   earnest ears for
amazing furnace   twilight's tale

k

Like the soap

which forgives tne garment's sin
in the magnanimity of foam,

The sun clears dark shadows
of the terror of the night;
stagnant pools are stirring again

with a fresh census of surging minnows.
The road's muddy kindness
has caked into crimson feast
in the solar kitchen of a centred sky:

toemarks embrace the streets, toe
marks which found their name
in the clayey book of lettering gallops.
For noontide is kiln for supple dreams
reared out of the dew's un

easy womb; running days
have cut their molar: noonwaves·
savour the nut of cracking truths ...
But heated arguments snake out into rainy concords:
and then another clay, then another dream –
like streets fore-giving their shadows.

i

I long for open spaces
After so many seasons in the belly of a myth,
Unlettered by blind legends, lost in
The labyrinthine syntax of unuttered proverbs

I long for open spaces
After the tongue's wordless wanderings
In the cave of the mouth, and lips
Which mourn the scar of keyless locks.

I long for open spaces
From edicts which thicken like medieval jungles
And streets which stumble their days
On nights of adamantine orders

I long for open spaces
Like a clearing in the forest
Like a stroll by the sea
Like the bird's blue range in the amplitude of the sky
Like mountains, like rivers,
Like echoes giving back the voice of talkative hills

I long for open spaces
From walls which squeeze the room with concrete claws
And doors which stiffen their hinges
Like sentries from forgotten epochs

I long for open spaces
From smiles which sting like jilted scorpions,
The hidden trap in the track of power hunters
Crimson tantrums in the festival of the knife

I long for open spaces
For a sun which springs from a sea of shadows
For the eye which unbinds the sky
In infinite visions

I long for open spaces

VI
Midlife

Midlife
now, and the sun so high in the centre of the sky
blue with space, eloquent with the aluminium laughter
of ample fringes,

a hazy patch sneaks across the expanse
once upon a cloud, humped with care
like pilgrims prospecting for rain

and shadows thick like a vow, so short
in the lofty dialogue of hurrying heels, define
the sturdy profile of noonsome dreams

the springy gait, the confident dash,
ligaments which love their bones, the neck
which bears its head like a happy burden

* * *

Midstream
where seasoned fins unfetter the fish,
my eyes a shoal which knows the purple song
of the bait,

the eel's tricky compass, and the blind appetite
of the crocodile which plunders the folds
with a brain unkindly small;

here, the quiet energy of seasoning waters,
past the tumbling infanthood of the cradle
of distant mountains;

not yet the snaky crawl in the aprons
of the mastering sea, an echo forever lost
in the mangrove's untutored beard

* * *

Midway
beyond the streets, where crossroads
dribble the feet: a thousand paths lie
open, still, in the infinity

of waiting guests: the dust is an armada
of eyes, stubborn hills lace their breath
with oceans of rippling sweat;

but in the alluvial laughter of mellow plains,
dreams thrive like pumpkins in the moon
of whispering showers

* * *

Midflight
the weaverbird serenades the sun,
a throbbing straw between its beak;
the forest bursts out

a medley of dancing leaves; noontide
is memory of ripening feathers, of nests
swinging below the palms

like testicles of giant clocks, quick
with exuberant nestlings, impetuous pupils
in the school of eloquent heights

* * *

Midthrob
the drum, its open hide doctoring
the wounded silence of unmediated scars
cicatriced in the dark groves

of groping dawns, coerced by palmless hands,
flogged by the fury of headless sticks;
the leather's wizened idiom

is a muffle threshing noontide for a tongue of fire;
the wood frail, still, from the termite of old twilights
seeks new timbre

in the forest of rapid seasons. Here now the gathering
of other legs, urging new tunes from
the sunlight of new accents.

* * *

   Midlife
and the sun so high in the sky of
unsparing seasons, coupling Want with Need,
Work with Labour, pain with acute pleasure,
probing sacred myths, dreaming new answers to old questions:

old questions to new answers, tracing every thread
in the seam of History's garment, screening every sheath
for the secret of boastful swords, firm on shifty grounds,
asking tall questions from ungentle giants

founding new hearths, roofing new homes,
stretching old lines from the legend of new loins,
moulding new ingots in the furnace of old suns,
beam between two shadows, (im)mortally long.

Visions and re-visions
and lingering squints straightened out by the vigilance
of mellowing pupils, the moon's milky jolt,
hills whose peaks plead for sharper vistas

Visions and re-visions
and shadows falling back like nimble masks,
hostile smiles, endearing frowns, rungless ladders,
nights set ablaze by the energy of sunny winds

Vision and re-visions
the ocean, one drop of bitter water,
eternity rolled out into the urgency of a wink.
Noons' laughter is a landscape severely rich.

Midlife

I have seen fire, I have seen rain
I have watched thin showers comb the grass
in the savannah of lean moons;
I have heard a scorched earth sizzle
at the touch of inchoate dew

I have seen roots touching roots in distant depths
far from warring trunks, away from the compound
pandemonium of rasping leaves;

I have climbed the sun's mountain and spied
milky marvels in the valley of the moon

I have seen smiles vanishing so fast
in the wilderness of the lip
I have seen brave benedictions which never veer
beyond the tongue
I have seen prayers twine into vipers

in the darkling jungle of slippery faiths;
I have seen friendly butterflies
sting more craftily than lurking scorpions:
I assay another look at Caesar's back,
And I see the yawning terror of unanticipated daggers

But Life's elegy is also an anthem of Hope:
for every waning fire, a blaze of a thousand flames;
the murderer's axe surprises innocent skulls
in the golgotha of crimson twilights, but dawn
will meet no swansong in the threshold of our lips

Dawn gave me a ring of eloquent stone
Noon will not turn it brass on my finger

    Midlife
then in a continent repressed into dire childhood
like *Sogolon's** child, crawling at eighty;

---

*   in *Sundiata: an Epic of Old Mali* by D. T. Niane

still struggling to count her fingers'
her grey gums toothless with tardy vowels,
her dark silence, her verbless eruptions,
her blanched rainbows, her truncated dreams
and the winds whispering through the trees,
their cheeks whip-marked and utterly sad;
and the storms mangling the dunes,
the Sahara one ocean of weeping sands,
and mountains, pledging ancient peaks,
to indulgent clouds, so scared of roaring plains.
Nights swap garments with days,
the sun staggers into the parlour of an overripe morning,
having slept too long in the chambers
of clever clouds.

The lion has lost its claws
to cheetahs of other forests;
what use, the magnificent mane
of emasculated tantrums

>   They who have heads have no caps
>   Those who have caps are in need of heads

My continent is a sky ripped apart by clever crows,
awaiting the suturing temper of a new, unfailing Thunder

But tell me, Africa,
Tell me more about this eternal childhood.
I have washed my hands in rivers
of many seasons:
I can now share the feast of ancient wisdoms
I have cut my teeth in forests of sturdy ivory,
ripening cornfields drive no fear into my jaws.

    Midlife
now Africa, beholding you, full-length, from shoulders
baked strong by your black sun;
my hands towards the sky, feet towards the sea,
I ask you these with the urgency of a courier
with a live coal in his running palm:

> The skeletal song of Zinjanthropus,
> was it a lie?
>
> The awesome ruins of Zimbabwe,
> were they fiction?
>
> The bronze marvels of Benin, of Ife,
> were they a lie?
>
> Is the Nile really a fickle tear
> down the cheeks of unmemorable sands?
>
> The geometry of your idoms, the algebra of your proverbs,
> were they sad calculations of pagan mouth?

My question, Africa, is a sickle, seeking
ripening laughters in you deepening sorrows

Giving, giving, always giving,
scorched by the Desert, blanched by the Sea,
bankrupted by the Sun, indebted by the Moon,
robbed of your tongue, bereft of your name

Giving, always giving
ebony springboard for giants of crimson heights

Giving, always giving
my memory is the thrashing majesty of the Congo
its dark, dark waters fleeced by scarlet fingers
its shoals unfinned, its saddled sands
listening earlessly to the mortgaged murmurs
of ravished ores.

Giving, always giving
the tall lyric of the forests
the talkative womb of the soil
the mountain's high-shouldered swagger
pawned, then quartered, by purple cabals.
The elephant's ivory is a tale of prowling guns,
the crocodile mourns its hide on the feet
of trampling gods

Giving, always giving
fiery dawns once wore you like a robe, oh Congo,
soft, warm, gracious like the cotton laughter
of Lumumbashi,
the Niger, the Volta, the Benguela
bathed the rippling hem of your luminous garment;
the sky was your loom, April's elephant grass
your needle with a hundred eyes;
your thread was the lofty spool of the eagle,
the chalky string of the egret in the dusty shuttle
of meticulous harmattans

And now noon
with the sun so young in the centre of the sky,
that robe is a den of dripping fragments
awaiting the suturing temper of a new, unfailing Thunder

Giving, always giving,

the drums are silent now, their lips bleeding
pale in the slaughtery of iron fingers;
decreed their idioms, their legend roundly mocked
by a cargo of plastic sticks:

> Bàtá* coughs out a muffled plaint,
> the *Fontonfron*** lacks knowing ears for
> its pensive proverbs
> the *kùkùǹbákù's**** throb staggers
> along the valley, falling back to dust
> like a wingless echo.
> The wood abhors its skin,
> orphaned couriers crouch gracelessly
> in the smutty saga of silenced squares,
> taunted by the eunuch laughter of swindling winds;
> idle legs haul lame curses at the maddening moon
> In these seasons of sundering silence
> how can the Towncrier hide his gong
> in the vanity of seedless clouds?

The night is cold with fright,
white with the simpering laughter of deracinated teeth
a crow describes shrill stunts in the magnitude
of the sky,
one with the night, one with the wordless clatter
of starless regions.
Which firefly will sow a little twinkle

---

*   a Nigerian drum
**   a Ghanaian drum
*** an African Drum of unknown origin

in the infinite furrows of a loamy darkness,
which gallant noon will define itself
by the black plenitude beyond a snoreless slumber?
The night is chill,
a sepia sun gathers strength behind the clouds,
mustering keen faggot for the pneumonia
of the moon.

A tropical truth unfurls the forests
sandal-less now, and club-footed from primordial wanderings,
from the turbanned domes of savannah shrubs
to the Bible-boughed tracts of Christian jungles.
Here where towering conspiracies usurp the sun,
a leafy murmur entwines the ferns,
smarting like a constipated boil.

The *ìrókò**
counts lunar rings in the geometry
of its soul,
Ògànwó's root is a con-tour of anonymous scars.
Bled by the sun, bled by the moon, *Obeche*
endures the seasons in buckets of dripping sap,
yawning nights stagger into murky days,
the sun so high in the equinox of leafy heights

Grinning boughs have swallowed the sun:
forests grope their days in hurricanes
of alien lanterns.

---

* Ìrókò, Ògànwó, and Obeche are topical trees valued as timber.

Natal whimpers, untellable enormities,
the pygmy terrors of the Leopard of the Congo,
Twilight's Desire, perfidious appetite
of nameless monsters, Conradianly dark.
The Congo's buffalo cannot count the mysteries
between its horns,
octogenerian cobras flaunt virile fangs
in Zomba jungles
Yamousoukro is a seething den of cannibal reptiles.

Grinning boughs have swallowed the sun,
for how long will the forest grope its days
in hurricanes of alien lanterns?

> My question, Africa, is a sickle, seeking
> ripening laughters in your deepening sorrows.

Quartered mountains, divided rivers,
lakes which plead their names in imperial rosters;
antelopes so scared of the eloquence
of their heels;
the savannah lies surprised by echoing thunders
of passing hoofs,
of empires falling before they rise,
and purple orders declining the noun
of waning crowns

In the after-dust of pompous gallops,
in the narrow conjugations of wild epochs,
their showy shadows remain, who squander
Guinea gold from grassland to desert kingdoms;
their showy shadows remain, grinning surrogates
of severe masters.

The baobab's breasts flip-flop in a merciless wind;
there is an impudent smile on the lips
of millet fields;
the locust bean swells its trail
with a redolent pomp.
Here every grass knows its verse in
the arduous litany of jealous gods

In the deciduous laughter of wounded winds,
under the perforated umbrella of a battered sky,
droughts yields place to floods,
locust blankets black out the sun
and fledgeling fields are sad like leprous stumps.
The uneven ribs of Africa ex-rayed
on Hollywood screens,
in gleeful concerts with unhappy tunes

But around a river's bend,
between spreading mountains and tricky rapids,
an epoch once shone like a nugget
unearthed by learning, burnished by
the dew-fresh mathematics of seeking minds.
History's melodrama is rife with interludes
of tonic laughters.

>   My question, Africa, is a sickle, seeking
>   ripening laughters in your deepening sorrows

>   Midlife

in a continent so ancient and so infant,
crawling, grey, in the scarlet dust of twilight horsemen,
ravished by the gun, crimsoned by ample-robed
natives and their swaggering fangs;

our sun so black with crying hopes,
wounded by the boundless appetite of hyena
rulers

Shorter every inch than our tower of dreams,
their eyes smugly sitting in the blind pit
of their funeral stomachs;
eunuch between the moons, their claws
gore-deep in assassinated wombs;
they whose fathers, whose fathers' fathers
emptied whole epochs into slaving galleons
have pledged once more the eulogy of the chain,
their hearts crammed with rums, fickle mirrors
and other gifts unremittingly Greek.
A keen-eyed sun shouts from the middle
of a drifting sky:

> Who will cure Africa's swollen foot
> Of its Atlantic ulcer?

My question, Africa, is a sickle, seeking
ripening laughters in your deepening sorrows

VII
Thread in the loom

m

Teller of tall tales
measured in lofty darings and mirrors which
tease the beard of phantastic skies,
beyond heights beyond depths,
beyond lateral fictions which compass the world
like navigated truths,

Beyond facts, beyond figures,
beyond seeming prisons where copyscapes
rule the lore like feigning dragons,
beyond stone walls of regimented shrouds
beyond spectre-cles of borrowed glitters

    Let the masquerade dance now
    in the metaphor of wordless probings

What is, is, is not
the feathered arrow of the mind's bird
laying eggs, softening stones into songs,
of muscular tones endowing waiting wood
with faces and opening breaths

Of shapes and shuttles
of the dappled yawn of the sky
which lost its rainbow to the gathering sea;
of heads which wear the shoe
of feet which don their caps
like accomplished fops

    * * *

What is, is, is not
like the long tale which twines into serpents
in the dark, dark jungle of the teller's mouth

Like burning river, like a season's showers
toughening into merciless *bílálà**
on the terraced farm of eating chiefs

Like a monkey who strolls down the hall,
complete with coat and bowler hat

Like the dead breaking through tear-soaked coffins
to mend their graves

Like the testicle of the tyrant inflated
in every street like yuletide balloons
of playing children

Like a kite dissolving into myriad ashes
in the house of the sun, then falling down
to earth like an orchard of playful birds

What is, is, is not
Cock-nouns chase hen-verbs,
the pen staggers across the page,
its nib mellow with migrant truths

The song stands in the marketplace,
breathing bread, breathing bullets

---

* leather whip

Let the masquerade dance now
in the metaphor of wordless probings

ii

Trees which join leaves will form a forest
rivers which join beds will form a sea;
if a cocky hen dares an army of roaches
it will not go back without a wounded beak.
I am a long, sharp knife emboldened by the sun
I glide clean and clear through the jungle of wax

What burden has shortened the tortoise's neck,
ask the river, ask the rock
ask the hard, hard tale of its old, old back

What sneaky wrath stole the snake's legs
ask the tree, ask the grass
ask the crispy fruit at the edge of the branch

What red labour provokes the termite
ask the clay, ask the clan
ask the anthill's chambers by the long, sad road

What end awaits the foraging fire
ask the patience of water
what fate awaits the brooding shadow
ask the straightening stature of the noontide sun

Man-slaying monsters
man, slaying monsters
man slaying monsters

o

I behold

Stubborn roots in league
against the sickle's insistence

The fireflames of mountains
which burn with volcanic splendour

I behold

The unwinding loincloths of men who play god
in temples of wooden angels

The deciduous laughter
of eating chiefs

I behold

The heaviness of the needle,
the weightless truth of fractured visions

The ringing alpha of concluded minds,
the sprouting song of buried virtues

I behold

The plough's glare in the mirror
of the preening soil

seasons stark drunk
on the talent of the grape

I behold

Stars marching back to claim
the patrimony of the night

The revelry of the new moon,
thunder's laughter in the comedy of the sky

I behold

Touching boulders,
The sympathy of stone.

Clouds which full-fill
the promise of rain

p

But what if we forget the past
And the past never fails to remember us ...?

I have left toeprints in the laughter
of fragrant dust,

wayfarers, do not dig my heels for rodents,
there is a quarry of gold in the pit of my sole.

Touched, touching,
I have hawked steaming songs

in streets of hungry ears,
broken the emperor's sword at its gilded hilt.

For me the orphaned cravings of the lone, unshirted child,
the out-cast, the road-bug, the forlornly wild

For me the last, last whistle of the train of night
of seafarers threatened by the appetite of the shark

For me the farm-boy's *alámọ̀** in the echoes of dust,
the mother's desperate sweat with the fever of an only child

For me tears which share the borders
of waiting laughters

---

*   a multi-toned, episodic ballad

For I am a stubborn thread in the loom of being
Indigo song, yarn of purple weftings

    I
 wear the sun's sweat like a garland of blue harvests
I am the caller at noon.

www.ingramcontent.com/pod-product-compliance
Lightning Source LLC
Chambersburg PA
CBHW011719220426
43663CB00017B/2909